What I Ask

What I Ask

Poems by

Marjorie Moorhead

© 2024 Marjorie Moorhead. All rights reserved.
This material may not be reproduced in any form, published,
reprinted, recorded, performed, broadcast,
rewritten, or redistributed without
the explicit permission of Marjorie Moorhead.
All such actions are strictly prohibited by law.

Cover design by Shay Culligan
Cover image by Marjorie Moorhead
Author photo by Marjorie Moorhead

ISBN: 978-1-63980-574-7

Kelsay Books
502 South 1040 East, A-119
American Fork, Utah 84003
Kelsaybooks.com

for
Rob, Max, John
Martha, Barbara, Nancy

4th Friday Poets

Also by Marjorie Moorhead

Every Small Breeze

In My Locket

Survival Part 2: Trees, Birds, Ocean, Bees

Survival: Trees, Tides, Song

Acknowledgments

Grateful acknowledgment goes to the editors of the following journals in which these poems first appeared, sometimes in earlier versions.

Amethyst Review: "If It Is Possible," "We Think We Step Alone," "Whisper," "Who Stopped?"
Literary North Constellation: Ekphrasis: "The Ladies"
The Poet's Touchstone: "I Meander, What Is the Measure?," "Poem Inspired by First Line of 'River Roads'"
The Rising Phoenix Review: "Turtle Island Microfiber," "(Villanelle) For My Planet"
A River Sings (Indolent Books): "Looking for Answers"
Sheila-Na-Gig Online: "Bedazzled," "Beyond the Pale," "Peonies," "Things we carry . . ."
Tiny Seed Literary Journal: "Dear Earth," "Returning Tide"
Verse-Virtual: "Any Day's Treasure," "Catching My Eye," "Enough Is Enough," "In my wildest," "In a Minor Key," "Into Morning," "Let Me Let Go Enough," "Tree, Be My Arms," "When I Love Trees the Most," "Wild and Free"
Writing In a Woman's Voice: "Cycle," "Shared Space"

Gratitude to the editors of these anthologies, in which the following poems first appeared.

A Change of Climate (Sam Illingworth & Dan Simpson ed.s, 2017): "Wandering the Anthropocene"
Thin Places & Sacred Spaces (Amethyst Press, Sarah Law, ed. 2024): "Summoning What Is Dear"

The following poems first appeared, possibly in earlier version, in these chapbooks:

Survival Part 2: Trees, Birds, Ocean, Bees (Duck Lake Books 2020): "The Agreement," "Beloved," "L'Amour Fou," "My Path," "Hampton Beach With Rob," "Horseshoe Crab," "Morning Walk," "Ocean Villanelle"
Survival: Trees, Tides, Song (Finishing Line Press 2019): "Hearing the Song"

I'd like to thank the editors/poets/readers who have read, responded to, and shared my work, and who enthusiastically share the work of others. An encouraging community is so needed in this world; we are all better for working together and listening to one another. I am grateful to have had exchanges with true poetry ambassadors and to have benefited from the generosity of those institutions and networks extending scholarship funds to those who need it.

Heartfelt thank you the wonderful poets who took time to consider these poems, and write their words for the cover.

Contents

Who Stopped?	17
United	18
Dear Earth,	19
Poets & Palm Seeds	20
Tree, Be My Arms	21
When I Love Trees the Most	22
Turtle Island Microfiber	23
Wandering the Anthropocene	24
Song of Rain	26
Do You Know What I Mean?	28
Soaring Grey	29
Beyond the Pale	30
Hearing the Song	31
The Agreement	33
Mid-September Loon	34
If It Is Possible	35
If Only I Could Snare You	36
Be the Moon	37
Smudge & Tangle	38
Waiting for that poem to come	39
Beloved	40
Ocean Villanelle	41
(Villanelle) For My Planet	42
Enough Is Enough	43
In a Minor Key	44
Warning	45
Shared Space	46
Whisper	47
At the End	48
Wild and Free	49
The Ladies	50
Maybe a Crow?	51
My Path	52

Any Day's Treasure (pantoum)	53
L'Amour Fou	54
Poem Inspired by First Line of "River Roads"	55
I Meander. What Is the Measure?	56
Looking for Answers	57
Let Me Let Go Enough	58
Into Morning	59
Things we carry . . .	60
Walk	61
Catching My Eye	62
Peonies	63
We Think We Step Alone	64
Signs	65
Should I become enveloped in loneliness	66
Born Into a Life	67
Carpe Diem	68
Like Those Chocolate Chips	69
Where I Stand	70
Morning Walk	71
Horseshoe Crab	72
Returning Tide	73
Pearl Lustered Kiss	74
Dusk	75
Hampton Beach with Rob	76
Summoning What Is Dear	77
Each Flower and Its Bee	78
Bedazzled	79
Twirling	80
In my wildest	81
Cycle	82
Post-It Note	83
What I Ask	84

*I picked up shells with ruby lips
That spoke in whispers of the sea . . .*

*. . . still I hear, from far away,
The blue waves breaking ceaselessly*

—Alexander Posey "Seashells" (1910)

*I am dazzled by the pure blue sky and glory sun,
just like anyone.
But, if I tell the truth,
cool shadow shade is more for me.
More silver than gold, calm rather than bold.
Just enough breeze in the air, teasing leaves to dance.*

Who Stopped?

Forgetting begins
when we leave
a world of beauty, belonging,
imagination;
tactile closeness to clouds,
the stars, the leaves;
as if there's no separation,
no distance to travel.
Reaching, reaching
yearning to touch, reunite.

We turn from the world that is a net;
a weave that holds us all,
all things.
Remember when you'd lie spread-eagle
looking at the sky,
and it was there for you,
rushed to meet you,
close as an embrace.
Who stopped hugging first?

United

We stand together, weathered
like the clapboards of an old barn.

Knots and nail holes,
patterns of wood showing through

paint that's been worn with honor
like a coat of fortitude,

sun bleached and rain battered,
witness to waves of snow and flowers.

Resolute, we are a faded, yet
fluttering flag.

Dear Earth,

You are the only nest I've ever known.
My shelter; my sustainer.

I have feathered and molted,
held in your palm.

In your forests, on your mountains,
at your shores, I have felt love, found calm.

I have given birth in faith that our home
will provide shelter and sustenance

to my offspring and theirs
and theirs and theirs.

Now, I worry dear Earth,
will you survive *us* and live on?

We've trod with heavy footstep
which you must spring back from.

With love and concern,
this human Mom

Poets & Palm Seeds

Poets float in my sky, a chosen constellation
soothing, reassuring, relating what it means
to be human on this planet, in this time,
in our bodies, beside others of our kind
and other species too, who live in our world
simply trying to survive, but also, to thrive.
We all want to thrive.
Not merely survive.
We all have to save one another;
stop stepping over each other
in our hurry to get . . . somewhere/something.
Checkering my zoom screen, beautifully varied poets,
each sharing words from their heart
about how we are human-at-the-edge-of-time.
In other words, how we are. How we are clinging
to a rapidly dying planet. The poets speak
of dolphin, they speak of cranes, of fox, of ice,
penguins, whales, coral reefs, the Milky Way.
Though gathered in hope, we are wet with tears.
My heart sinks low, heavy and pulsing.
The evening seems to plead with pressed palms.
Standing, I leave the desktop to wander a bit,
closing curtains as the sky grows darker,
looking longingly for a glimpse of our moon,
Super and Blue at the end of this month;
a gateway month, leading to change.
We feel it in the air tonight. I've seen it
written on leaves along my walking path.
Back in my seat now, focused on the screen,
Angela Torres reads her poem* about palm seeds
and harvesting the heart.

* "Harvesting the Heart" by Angela Narciso Torres

Tree, Be My Arms

Today, I let branches speak
for my heart and I let them
calm my mind as I depend
on the gentleness of apple blossoms
just blooming on our tree.
Light pink, barely a shade above
white, and the lime green of newness
draping each arm in ceremony.
Celebration of what is,
what might come to be,
and what will surely pass.
Tree, let me stand in your trunk.
Solid bark protecting a core.
Let me flow with the sap; a sweetness
that nourishes. I'll anchor in your roots
even as emotions soar.

When I Love Trees the Most

It's not when there are branched silhouettes
against the setting sun, highlighting
a pink and orange screen with mingled patterns.

Not even in Fall, when leaves,
in a coral reef display of color,
adorn hillsides with gold, orange, red bouquets.

It's not when trees are flowering,
sprouting with green, and newly built nests,
hosting the songs of Spring.

When I love trees the most, it's a cloudless sky,
at the turning from June to July,
sun so hot, even early in the day,

glasses slip down the bridge of my nose,
sweat trickling from eyebrows and tickling
a stream between shoulders to waist.

Merciful islands of shade, offered
from fully leafed branches above,
puddle between arid pavement deserts,

becoming oasis after oasis of cool.
As long as I see one ahead, I know
I'll make it, and be able to recover.

Lovely gracious trees, treasured
more than your beauty
is your grand generosity.

Turtle Island Microfiber

The radio tells me this morning,
in voices kind and concerned,

there are particles of plastic in Lake Champlain
so small, they can't be filtered by treatment plants.

Micro plastic trash they called it.
(*punk rock band* my ears amuse).

This plastic from fleece-wear
will merge with our food chain, is announced.

We will eat plasticated fish
from laundering our fine-threaded plastic shirts.

My son, visiting home from college, has my head spinning
trying to keep up with all his words for environmental and social
    tragedy.

Apparently, we are trying to repossess
ourselves of our humanity

away from psycho technology
in the Anthropocene.

I am glad his generation is trying
to figure it out because

I want my children, and theirs,
to know sparkling water that hosts creatures who

co-habit with us and provide sustenance
that is clean and pure.

Water they can dip their toes into and want to plunge further.
Nutritious air that lungs can consume with passion.

Will that story be a memory told,
of an ancient dream, of an island called "Turtle"?

Wandering the Anthropocene

LED lights flickering
Microwaves emitting

Surveilling satellites vie for air ways
With cell phone frequencies

Rubble and soot-filled air
Like the 9/11 toxins everywhere

Devastated environments
Endless wars; careless industries

Once thriving communities dying
Bleached coral; flattened Mosul

Plastics and nuclear isotopes
Failed reactors; failed states

Failure to thrive
Shrinking ice; drought; floodwater coursing

Created scarcity
Our byproduct of greed

Seeds genetically modified
Mismanaged soil toxically fertilized

Humans displaced
Species disappeared

Searching for authenticity
With freedom from techno-tyranny

Striving for existence reclaimed
Community found in terms un-dictated

Kickstart organic motivation
Individuals must make the proclamation

to flourish

Song of Rain

The birds were singing
a song of rain.
In their song I heard
beauty, and pain.
Birds sang the sound
of our story unfolding,
our round planet turning,
our joy, and our burning.
Piercing the air with heartbreaking clarity,
birds sang of love and charity
and also the pain of the lack
of that love;
of need, hunger, want—
manufactured disparity.
As I walked, the birds sang
a song of rain.
Of both cleansing, and sorrow.
And I thought,
how will we possibly make our way
through to tomorrow?
In the midst of our pain
but also unfathomable beauty,
are we capable of balance?
Sing, birds. Of rain. Of salvation.
Sing to our hearts
and wake up a nation
of humans who care.
It is high time to give a damn,
revere what is given to us as a home.
Walking earth as tenants, we're responsible
for maintenance, preservation.
The birds are singing a siren song.

A warning—a pulsing—a call to attention.
They're singing a ballad of love,
saying, *fix what is wrong.*
Only then might you flourish, in celebration!

Do You Know What I Mean?

The internet tells me today, mama Orca
is finally ready to frolic and play.
Her dead calf let go, to rot on the floor
of an ocean that failed her.
Not enough salmon around. No magic potion
found to change things back
to ways they once were. Abundant.

The internet tells me today, don't stay blue;
. . . even though climate change is true. Scroll technology
shows, troubles will come and they will go,
you needn't hold on to woe. There isn't anything to do;
surf infinite sites, waves of clicks and bytes.

A mother who grieved for seventeen days,
has laid her calf to rest at ease. Starved daughter
atop her head; corpse borne seventeen nights.
The mourned body sinks to decompose,
following death-at-sea funeral rites.

Mama Orca rejoins a shrinking pod. One member less.
Salmon found, they'll survive for now. Don't think
about the why's or how to fix this mess.
Don't think of your role. Go on with your life.
Online in your phone, float in a cloud, all needs met.

Scroll. Scroll. Issues arise and fade on the internet.
Maybe taking a selfie will help you forget
baby Orca whale, dead. Don't pause for regret.
Elephants endangered; starving bears.
No fret; swipe when seen.
Disappearing ice, flooding and fire; dismissed.
Do you know what I mean?

Soaring Grey

Birds of a feather flocked together,
right over my head yesterday.
Grey, folded origami shapes open and closed,
fluttering against a steel blue sky.
I walked, and they circled, up in the wind,
near treetops edging the wood. Joyous,
symphonious, they soared,
skimming along edges of the clouds.
Below, non-feathered and cold, thinking of tasks
to be done, I wondered, where is my cohesive
group? Co-flyers on an uplifting current?
Where my cohorts of shared experience and need?
Why aren't we flying together, in pattern,
like the undulating shapeshifting cluster of crows
witnessed one morning, just before dawn;
their caws a crackling cacophony.
None were left behind.
Those that broke pattern were scouts who returned,
welcome in the winged fold to share whatever they'd learned.
What were they saying? If only I knew, it might be a clue
to inclusive collective; how to behave
that's not isolation, blinders on, head down, boxed in a cubicle.

Beyond the Pale

Woe is the coral reef
who chokes in damaged waters.
Imagine trying to breathe
in a house of smoke.
Imagine being caressed by poison
palms; embraced by toxic arms
and there's no escape.
Imagine you've graciously
housed visitors from all walks, all ways,
sheltered in your corridors, welcomed
in the nooks and crannies; a community
of travelers whose paths crisscross, interwoven
to create a sustaining fabric for all,
but your place is invaded and the life choked out.
Bycatch and ghost gear bring ruin.
Host and provider no more, you cannot
survive relentless siege and plunder.
Bleached to a white surrender, you sway
unhealthy now in an alien galaxy
of floating forever plastic.

Hearing the Song

Deep red cardinal in a tree,
like a sailor in ship's crow's nest.
Piercing notes from open throated song
float to changing winds at his chest.
Red cardinal—do you know White Rhino is gone?
Sudan, last male of his breed.
Will you sing him a monody, mark his passing
in your prosody, the sounded urgency we need?

Painted Sea Anemones, afloat in currents
off British Columbia, nutrient-fed by ocean's
forceful swells, multi-colored below the surface blossoms
on display, like a flower-shop's vibrant bouquet.
They share an ocean with Great Pacific Garbage Patch
(GPGP), a trash vortex, between Cali. and Hawaii.
Riding a gyre, bright colored plastic shards
and fishing nets form this multi-pieced barge,
looming as an island of debris.
If, like surface-coating oil, dark and slick,
it shadowed the bouquet anemones, who'd sing
their elegy, lament their getting sick?

An elephant gives birth surrounded by others circling in
to protect the calf. A fortress of swinging trunks,
wide flat hooves, flapping grey ears, wrinkled skin.
Do they sense extinction lurking? Like white rhino Sudan,
will they vanish too, in coming years?
New England has lost Eastern Cougar. Vanished. Gone. *Ghost Cat.*
Our Catamount/Puma/Mountain Lion will never again be seen.
Species' extinction is rampant. Imagine that. An escalating crisis
of the Anthropocene.

High atop tree boughs, red cardinal trills, claiming
his spot in a wild chorus singing Earth's praises.
Red-brown mate, in carefully crafted cup-nest,
joins, with her own lyric phrases.

We should listen to cardinals' song. Elephant's ways.
Anemones being nourished in ocean's currents.
Pray over vanished rhino's bone.
Remember the roars of big cats who perish.
We cannot exist on this planet alone.
We should listen. We should cherish.

The Agreement

You give me sunshine; your optimism
I give you Place. Grounded stability.
You provide levity, adventure, propelling action.
I take care of detail, routine, the repeated minutiae
of sustainability.

A balancing act in flux; we are symbiotic partners.
We'd best opt for protection;
our habitat is measured; proportionally equal.
Balanced like the yin/yang symbol,
neglect could extinguish us
causing death
by Disparity.

Mid-September Loon

We were witness to a Loon conversation on the lake.
Heard their thrilling voices! saw their give-and-take.

We wandered in the field across from the water;
took a run along the road. Views of mountains, trees

and meadow, notes of season's changing mode.
Golden Rod creeping in, starts to crowd out Queen Anne's Lace.

Resting on a bench at the coarsely sanded beach, looking
at leaf-strewn water. Golds and oranges undulate on a sun-glinting
   surface.

Together, we enter the lake. I wade only waist-deep;
he quickly dives under. Then, we hear them talking, calling out to
   each other.

One rises up, flapping its wings at the reflecting water,
white belly exposed, using indescribable language.

An answer comes back, haunting in its flutey uniqueness.
Did they know we were there, in their home, sampling pleasures?

Did they care? Such a startling glimpse, looking
in a mirror of coexistence;

our shared, spectacular world,
enchanted with wild and ancient spirits.

If It Is Possible

Searching for sunrise this morning, east
through freckled patches of window screen.
A quiet yellow glow appears, mellow, serene,
not heart-gripping dramatic pinks we're sometimes shown,
so arresting it feels that one could die happy, now complete,
having been immersed in such a thing.
I switch to west, our back window view over the river,
glistening like diamonds, and there comes a faint pink-purple
blush, underlining the full Wolf Moon, vivid in this waking sky.
Small but powerful, our moon at its apogee, glowing at me
like a round white grape lit bright from within.

If it is possible to pilot one's way into a day,
best way is with full moon above a river, color in the sky,
and a root centered in openness; allowance for come-what-may.
To be nimbly accepting the rough, easy, or arresting,
received softly as massaging, hugging, holding your heart
with the astonishment of wonder.

If Only I Could Snare You

A tree points out, and I try to capture,
the elusive moon. Moon easily escapes
my feeble camera, not fit for the caper.
Tree points its branch strategically,
tip touching the small, smoke-white floating disk
hiding as a cloud yet unable to blend in completely,
its distinguished glow too luminous
to be camouflaged as lolling mist.

You there, Director of ebb and flow,
toss me a crumb, Maestro!
Pale and cratered saltine cracker,
why do I wish to lure you down, into this soup of lunacy?
Is escape from dread a fantasy?
All efforts to lasso fail. If only I could snare you
moon, I could share you,
and the feelings of awe and wonder you inspire
that soothe the soul and bring me out, far and wider
than this small world in which I flounder
tossed by worry, distress, anxiety, contemplating crumbling
ending of all around me, sometimes violently, sometimes subtly.

Moon, with a hug, with a share, possibly dread could be diluted.
Or, am I awestruck, dazzled, deluded?

Be the Moon

My morning newspaper headline says
Polar Bears Are Top of the Food Chain.
The article reports a human mother and her young
son were killed in an "attack."
The big bears see us as food.
Usually, they prefer seals.
But occasionally, a human looks like a meal.
And, they maul.
Life can be snatched away.
In the flash of a bomb.
In the pierce of a bullet.
By the claws of a bear.
I want to live being aware.
Remembering how precious existence really is.
Not to live in fear.
To honor the bear,
the earth, the sky, the moon, the loon.
To be not-apart.
Tai chi teacher says wear the moon for a hat.
And, we do! All of us. Seen or not, we do
—until the day it is swiped off,
by bear, by illness, by old age.
Be the bear. Be the moon. Be the river.
Walk as though on river ice—with care and intention.
Be brave. Find balance, strength in grace.
I will try to remember these things
and carry them into each day
as I rise to see sun's pink rose held by the clouds.

Smudge & Tangle

Layered, like a ball of rubber bands
criss-crossed, hugging each other to center,
we're a smudge and tangle

of lines and smears, laughter, tears.
A smudge and tangle of struggle,
determination, stumble & grace.

Traces of motion, tracks, connections, left
like contrails, or shimmery paths painted by snails.
Imprints of agency, intention, itinerary, direction.

Like scurrying chipmunks & squirrels, birds & bees
swirling, rabbits bounding, insects flying, spiders weaving
webs, we smudge and tangle, morphing

like starlings in murmuration,
like crows in a murder. Dispersing, then gathering.
Undulations scattering and collecting, herding.

The forest stays connected underground
laced with mycorrhizal fungi.
A tree's crown needs the soil at its base.

We're together, clinging, rooted, linked
to one another. A woven net, we are one,
tangled, even when we think we move alone.

Waiting for that poem to come

but it is caught in the clouds
behind my eyes.

Thick as the fog that hovers heavy
above Mascoma river, just downhill.

I see it in the mornings now,
first look out our back window.

A floating greyness
ubiquitous

ominous?
wetting all it touches,

all that waits quietly,
patiently, for the sun.

Beloved

Glittering water; glittering sand.
A sound that will not end.
Waves, relentless in their return; ceaseless.
Each freshly formed, cresting in a gallop
of white foam, racing to shore.

You don't wish it to end;
the rush and fizzle and hiss.
Like schuss of skis on an endless mountain,
cars whooshing by on a highway to forever,
wind in the trees of a storm.

Its absence would be horror.
This rhythmic drone that is head-filling, repetitive;
telling you: "wake-up"; "wake-up."
Its hum a soothing lullaby,
singing: "let go, relax"; "let go, relax."

Are the fish hearing this beautiful song?
Possibly, below ocean's surface they hear their own.
Different from our melody above,
but as beloved.

Ocean Villanelle

It's the sound that I love; it speaks to me.
A song of connection,
reminding of eternity;

of death and return. The song of the sea;
singing a tune of perpetual motion.
It's the sound that I love. It speaks to me;

the hiss and slurp, the whooshing plea
of wave after wave making commotion,
reminding of eternity.

Walking along beach trails, relaxed and free,
this melody woos like a magnetic potion.
It's the sound that I love; it speaks to me.

A feeling of wonder and mystery
provoking awe; each minute detail, perfection;
reminding of eternity.

Each grain of sand, seashell, weed, anemone;
every swelling blue-green hue, offering satisfaction.
Ultimately, it's the sounds that I love; they speak to me,
reminding my soul of eternity.

(Villanelle) For My Planet

Treat your home with love; it will sustain you.
Unattended, webbing can tear.
A net's weave is strong when its connections are true.

Our actions have changed things more than we knew.
We haven't treated our surroundings with care.
Treat your home with love; it will sustain you.

Stories are told using many a hue;
facts about deeds not always laid bare.
A net's weave is strong only when its connections are true.

The lies we were told by greedy oligarchs grew.
Their practice of depletion and pillage for profit, not fair.
Treat our home with love; it will sustain you.

Let us rip open the veil and see through.
We need all be invested in our habitat's fare.
A net's weave is strong when its connections are true.

Time has come for action that's new.
Create stewardship in which we all have a share.
Treat Home with love; it will sustain you.
A net's weave's as strong as it's connections are true.

Enough Is Enough

Two Volcanoes Rumble Into Action in Russia's Far East
—APnews.com, 11/20/2022

War rages and ravages, and
the round Blue Planet bursts into protest.
Long-seething volcanoes begin to erupt.
I will cause a roiling rumble of my own, Earth says.

Perpetrators of pollution and plunder:
Your callous violence spews noxious
toxins from weaponry and destruction.
You want to kill? then I shall show you death
at a scale beyond your ken.
Red hot lava bleeds down my thighs
to cover you in flame.
Your hideous, imperious, murderous ways
shall be the limit to your days. I will bury you
in shame.

In a Minor Key

Melancholy's in the air; sweet sadness,
like a Richard Thompson song.
Thimble berries, ripe for picking;
acorns on the ground.
Clouds sail in, this late August morning,
like ships to another land.
That song sings in my head and heart now;
stuck, swirling 'round and 'round.

Autumn seeps in, like a lazy fog bank
cloaking hillsides, and river's edge.
Echinacea's petals point down to stems now,
laid flat, like ears of some purple hound dog.
Centers exposed like so many noses, lifted up to sniff the air.
These flowers seem umbrellas turned inside-out now,
or badminton birdies batted, then landed on the ground.

Age claws in, quietly, like a bird nest robber,
fur-coated, sharp-toothed, stealing away unprotected youth.
We've danced and danced 'til feet drag on the ground.
Turns out, marionette strings control our movements;
twirl things upside-down. As blue Earth turns toward winter,
will anything, *like song? like love?* be enough to save us;
be enough to turn the world around?

Warning

The sky is broken,
holding bad air.
The air is poison,
saturated with waste
—thrown from fire.
Fire in forests north of here.
Particles carry on currents of air,
tides of our atmosphere.
We are fish in a bowl of oxygen
above, gravity below. We live
in a terrarium we have poisoned
with waste. Altered the natural order.
Off balance, we shake the snow globe,
our bubble, and have to live in the turmoil
of particle storms and swirls, blanketed
in a communal quilt of angst.

Breath has been a given gift,
something we had with expected ease
but now is reneged—made conditional.
Stop messing with me Earth warns,
or your air will not flow smoothly
in and out of your lungs. It will need a filter.
A cleaning. You must keep house
better than this.

Shared Space

Ask me why I'm so drawn to the bird feeder
outside our back window.
I'll start telling you of big bluejays,
cherubic chickadees, clumsy-beaked cardinals,
finches, nuthatches, wrens and even woodpeckers
who appear, eager for black oil sunflower seeds
hung in a tube with holes and perches.

Looking out, I am lost in feathers and swoops,
satisfied hunger and cooperative-acceptance-of-other
in shared space.
Not like our news headlines.
Stories focused on divisiveness,
violence, need, exploitation . . . greed.

The birds don't want ALL the food.
They want to be fed, just like the rest of us.
Somehow, they manage to attend to need side by side,
or in turn, yellow feathers near blue. Red feathers near brown.
Black caps and tufted together, co-existing.

Whisper

When sky is baby blue
and the clouds mirror newly fallen snow,

white fluffs clean and crisp,
tucked in around all edges, a comforter

matching robin's egg, and the trees,
who whisper to each other

constantly, trunks gently swaying,
branches bare, but not brittle,

what are they saying?

At the End

I am telling you now,
with the rhythm
of my rippling,
and the wink of my glinting surface
as it turns along a serpentine route,
the red berries blazing nearby
and the bronzed leaves,
tear-drop shapes pointing toward earth.
Fallen leaves as well, tell you
with their dry crackle
and pungent smell and flutter
when tickled by a breeze.
The breeze tells you too, as do newly bared branches
it is flowing through. As does the sky above,
today truly, serenely blue.
Are you listening? Are you joining in the saying
We are here, all together.
Flutter, flow, ripple, glow, crackle, glint, blaze.
Raise a ruckus, as a chorus.
Let all voices ring.
Hum, peck, chant, thrum.
Stomp and tromp, skip. Jump.
Fly. It is our time to sing.

Wild and Free

Give me wildflowers indiscriminate,
strewn across a field, flecked promiscuously
through blades of grass, playful; free.

Give me that, over planned and curated
garden flowers maintained;
robust and beautiful yet oh so groomed
and special. Isolated in designated territories,
separated by policing mulch, every one in its place.

Give me wild and free and random.
Give me mixed and blended, mingling.
Bright blossoms of dandelion littered
like stars in a green night.
Sprays of blue forget-me-nots flowing
like a stream cascading.
Neatly fringed aster, light-purple petals
around yellow button center, swaying, singing
shoulder to shoulder in a big congregation.

Turn a corner; be surprised by joy; stunned
by the vibrant, speckled gift of a wildflower field's
abounding variety. Smells, leaves, petals;
texture, hue, pattern, beckoning
pollinator bees, butterflies, birds and beetles.

Indeed, a wild growing field invites
imagination's flow in yellow, purple, orange, pink.
Joy hops alongside as a happy rabbit leaping.
A wild growing field has my heart aflutter
in its heaving-sided, full-to-brim basket
of perennial love.

The Ladies

They sit, in a sacred circle of three,
exuding pure joy just to BE.

Celebrating each's presence;
sitting as garden gnomes,

cross legged, naked in all glory.
A pure connection to Earth

is the story they tell to any passerby.
Planted as they are on the ground,

like cabbages, lumpy and round,
one with arms raised to the sky,

their song of laughter
a pulse that beats in our chests.

Telling us, relax, rejoice,
we are all in our element.

Maybe a Crow?

An angel in the ice
of a melting river
as we walk along.
Maybe a swan;
a dove; a moth; a fairy?
White wings jutting up,
and I think about iconography,
climate change, and hope.
Salvation may insist in imagination,
mythology, and freedom of expression
to get out of the box;
the cage we're building,
holding us down
unfeathered and sinking
in an ice floating river.
Maybe it's a black crow,
high in the pine boughs,
who will know
where we go
from here.

My Path

My steps, a measured amble
of pleasure.
The sidewalks,
some black, some light,
strewn with acorns and their lids,
with leaves of many colors, sizes, shapes,
lined with grasses, tufting up from the cracks.

The sidewalks are my beach
at low tide.
I wade through them,
leaving foot prints as I go.
Striding through littoral gifts offered
by weather and season, coloring my journey,
dotting my path with treasure.

Any Day's Treasure (pantoum)

There's a walk I take, every day.
A regular route, uphill to reservoir and back.
I've been walking this walk for years.
When the sun has risen, chased away any fog, but shadows remain,

I head uphill to the reservoir
to feel centered, calm, and free.
When the sun has chased away morning fog, but shadows remain,
my precious time

to calm, feel centered and free.
The sidewalk stretches out, a path in front of me.
Precious time.
Pulse flowing from heart to limbs,

the sidewalk path welcoming me.
This repeated walk, my reliable pleasure,
coaxing flow from heart to extremity.
An every day walk, the jewel in any day's treasure.

L'Amour Fou

A crow, wingspan wide as a hawk's, glides to its landing
in the Maple branches. Purple iris display stately blooms.
Purple also, chive and clover sprout pompoms atop thin stems,
cheering on rhododendron's exploding magenta puffs.

High in the wind above, a bird call familiar to my ear.
Threee, threee; two-two-two-two is what I hear,
though it's not a sentence I comprehend.
My translation: meee, meee; you-you-you-you.
An imagined invitation to join a conversation in song.
No need to break the code. I hear:
threee, threee; two-two-two-two (meee,meee; you-you-you-you)
and respond happily, with an ode: *oui, oui!; true-true-true-true!*

Welcome shade is shrinking fast as I move, skipping, smiling,
navigating island to island of cooler air, gifted by tall trees,
in the sidewalk cosmos of this warm June morning.

Poem Inspired by First Line of "River Roads"

Let the crows go by hawking their caw and caw
—Carl Sanburg

Let the Chickadees sweep sweep
their ins and outs; swoop
tree to feeder, feeder to tree.
Let them do what small winged creatures do.
Dragonfly, butterfly, hummingbird, bee
travel through air as if waves of the sea.
How would it feel to be so free?

I connect with place through ground,
plodding a path. Let me stride stride sensing
each step is sacred.
An asking. A practice. Of opening.
Open open breathe breathe walk walk,
attaining the state of ease.
At peace, serene, immersed in the moment,
open to all, flourish to perish. This is a way
to cherish. Cherish.

I Meander. What Is the Measure?

The water, so needed, has come in a steady falling.
Its patter raincoats the day in a slicker of isolation.
As soil sponges swell with gratitude, slaking every fiber,
I wander, like a pollen dazed bee alighting on clover,
I meander through a thought field, veiled in mist.
The day floats by. One of those.
Ephemeral. Inconsequential. Nothing solid happens
in hours spent alone, thoughts strolling.
A cotton candy cloud day, full of fluff and air
and the stickiness of regret.
The feeling of *haven't done enough*.
Tasks gone untouched, goals unformed . . .
is it *lost time,* if unfolded away from any others?
No extending past the self, no offered helping hand.
Shall I give myself a pass, or fret? What is the measure
of worthiness? Life is not a performance—
does it need an audience?

Looking for Answers

I don't know exactly what a prayer is.
I do know how to pay attention, how to fall down
into the grass, how to kneel down in the grass,
how to be idle and blessed
—Mary Oliver, "The Summer Day"

Yesterday's walk—fish scale clouds.
Three woodpeckers calling loud,
flying tree to tree following one another.
What do you call a trio of good-omen birds in flight?
What do we name these clouds scaling through sky
in scalloped arcs like the shimmery
flat side of an ocean dwelling fish?

What do you call the feeling
when everything seems akimbo and in limbo;
really neither here, nor there.
Almost to Spring, yet temperatures still plummet
turning snowmelt to ice.
Almost at war; the world on edge.
Pandemic ravishes in places; is calming down in others.
Folks don't know what to do—mask and distance,
or step back to "normal."

I've fallen out of practice how to gather;
have settled back into hermitic ways,
finding comfort in alone-ness;
unease at the thought of "in-person."
What do we call it, to feel lost
in the midst of every day; in the midst of your life;
your precious life.

Let Me Let Go Enough

Slate gray river,
I saw you shining last night.

Don't know if it was comet or satellite,
but something hovered above you,

beaming bright. Your ripples were alive
with conversation.

What is it you and the stars discussed
while I lurked at our windows,

binoculars in hand, trying to read the mystery
as sleep evaded me in those hours when all is quiet,

when most are asleep, dreaming.
Seeking ease of mind, I take to peeping—

the night sky so full of wonder—permitting escape,
expansion, release from narrow parameters.

The riparian zone is far reaching,
as is the celestial one. There are really no borders

where we try to place them, wanting
to impose order that suits our desire for conquest.

My zone extends beyond the container of skin
and bones I call Body. If I liquify into ripples

like a river, I can flow, I can fly.
Last night I traveled to the stars, searching for peace.

Treading water in the glittering swells let me let go enough
to float into dawn.

Into Morning

At dawn,
the horizon fills with pink
then periwinkle.

A radiant peach glows behind the pines across our street.
Next, purple octopus stretches amethyst arms wide
and along the horizon-line of hills, rooftops and pointing trees.

Peach's glow, calming now, dissipates.
Ribboning lavender tentacles lay a path into this day's sky.
In a boat of assimilating colors, I watch, flowing into morning.

Things we carry . . .

get held in skin; melded to bones;
floated in marrow.
Bodies, bodies, they become like baskets
holding, holding the moments we've walked through.
A flavor seared on the tongue
stitches to place
or person in that moment
forever on.
Sound that went through chest as song,
now lingers always in every vein.
Seeing certain light diffused
in golden mist, a glow (as J.M.W. Turner painted),
soaks into our hearts like rain.
We carry our loads as blessing or burden, and become
a particular mix; a unique recipe. A precise bouquet;
the assortment—shapes, colors, leaves, stems—
of which flowers display and describe us

Which flowers display and describe us—
stems, leaves, colors, shapes—the assortment a precise
bouquet; a unique recipe; the particular mix we've become.
We carry our loads as blessing or burden,
soaking into our hearts like rain, in golden mist,
glowing, J.M.W. Turner-esque.
Light diffused, lingering, always now in every vein.
Sound that went through chest as song
or a person who, in that moment stitches to place;
a flavor seared on the tongue.
Holding, holding the moments we've walked through,
bodies, bodies, become like baskets.
Floating in marrow,
held in skin, melded to bones:
the things we carry . . .

Walk

It's Sunday
and my religion
is Walk.

Breathe.
Smell.
Listen.
Look.

Cathedral sky.
Wind, holy roller.
Birds, my congregation.

Its a dogma of wonder;
a practice of reverence;
a commitment to wholeness.

The big picture;
the weave of the net.

Catching My Eye

Imagine a church pew lady's glove.
White lacy upturned palm,

cupping bees and butterflies,
swaying gently on long stem,

leaves like feathers of a green bird.
Many tiny blossoms together

in a circle-burst of celebration
decorating hot July fields,

sharing wild ground with Bindweed,
Black-eyed Susan.

Call it "Queen Anne's Lace," "Bishop's Lace,"
"Wild Carrot," "Bird's Nest."

Call it summer time. Heat waving
off pavement. Fields buzzing alive.

Matured from tight cups to open parasols,
floating in the sun like lily pads on a glinting pond,

little flower-clouds. Clustered landing platforms
for pollinators who flit between these

blossom-spangled constellations
in the sky of their field.

Peonies

The Peonies, once pink-fisted baby's paws,
have opened wide. Proudly now, they celebrate

pink poise with luscious, strongly stated odor.
A flagrant fragrance; nothing to hide.

Mature blossoms so full and weighty they're pulled
to earth where ants board sweet petal planks.

A fleeting moment of time from tight balls budding
to blushing-cheeked potential, to becoming colossal,

intricately detailed blossoms, open and spilling
every secret; wide and so full

they propel their own arc of descent
down to the ground that nurtured them.

Oh, that my journey, and yours, could be so complete.
Joyful from first stages to last.

To leave that scent—unforgettable;
to live a life, generous; authentic—unregrettable.

We Think We Step Alone

We think we step on solid ground,
but shifting sands are all I've found.
Shadows and mist,
transforming cloud formations . . .

We gather together as a particular form
but nothing stays solid.
Nothing remains untroubled.
Not the body. Not thought.

We ought to have wings or at least carry,
at all times, one of those life preserver rings.
For flight; for buoyancy, something to cling to
in the storms of uncertainty.

Side by side, or across the globe,
you and I are droplets of the same foggy mist.
Hold hands with me, link arms.
Let us pool together awhile,

I'll splash in your puddle, and you in mine.
We'll soak heavy so all will sink, a weighty mix
running from us as rivulets, soaking
into common ground.

Signs

I wake looking for birds, waken as they faithfully
come to black oil sunflower seeds hung at our deck.
A path from tree to seeds beckons the feathered bodies
so that I might sink into soft tomato red, or wear
the black mask, or flit the blue tail, or lift bright tufted head.
Resting in their flight and feeding, I am nourished
for my day of two legged walking. Dogged plodding,
trying for acceptance of come-what-may.

I'll wait for the fog to rise, tree tops emerging.
I'll hope for the sun to highlight any determined leaves
remaining, and also those that surrendered and now surround
my footsteps on sidewalks layered with acorns, maple seed pods,
berries and nuts I can't name. A trail-mix whose ingredients
are signs of the season. Last blast bright colors that tell a tale
of pale to come, time of prescribed patience and quietude in grey
and blue. An interlude one must learn to endure by embracing
retreat, and letting feathers come to view.

Should I become enveloped in loneliness

I'd like to taste things as a child again.
To learn them for the first time.

Size; texture; flavor . . . drool.
Bring all I meet to mouth, connect

by yearning; learning by becoming intimate
with what's at hand. Exploration free

from preconceived notion, fear, or revulsion.
Am I willing to put a branch, leafy with lichen,

onto my tongue? Between my teeth?
To encounter all its aspects, crags and crevices

of bark's each inch, where rough and green
lacy-feathered meet—how—why.

Have we traded sensual interrogation
for pseudo representation? So lonely,

this virtual non-sensation sent back from a screen.
If I touch something fully, might it

then know me too?
Are we separate anymore?

Born Into a Life

Snug, this morning, in a home of my own,
not living on streets or a clearing in the woods.
I look out windows and watch the birds.

Dark Eyed Juncos have arrived.
Not pummeled by police, bombed, or robbed
of survival by calving ice, in this moment,

feeling fortunate to be alive.
Not something earned; nothing done
in particular to "deserve" my comfort.

Just a being, among many, born into a life
that is finite. Everything's born on a road to its end.
Along the way, fences to mend. A path to wend.

Dark Eyed Junco, out there pecking for food,
I salute you. I am happy to have met you.
Would you think the same of me?

Do I project any kind of beauty?
If I were feather-coated,
what would the pattern be?

Carpe Diem

People seize the day in different ways.
Some paddle kayaks out to meet with loons,
swim in a lake with ducks.
Others seek shade from trees, books in hand,
paper and pen, looking to read the clouds,
treasuring each breeze.
Lilies bloom their colors of fire.
Morning Glories beam a deep purple hue.
Hydrate, hydrate we urge each other,
taking care, carrying on. How to live a healthy life
on our heating planet that's dying?
Seeking nurture in the rain floods and heat waves,
we attend theater, opera, under a tent, applaud the orchestra,
dream of heightened love and passions. Fierce and feisty,
fated, like Carmen.

In a favorite poem, blue horses gather,
lower their heads together.
Graze in a cluster.
What do they know?
What do they know of doom?

Like Those Chocolate Chips

No matter the sidewalk is speckled in ice,
swathed in slush. No matter
our driveway a riverbed of mud and frozen tracks.
The sky has broken blue, once again.
The sun has risen and shines through
another morning. I can walk outside
in fresh air, choosing each step wisely, wending
my way, encouraging my heart
to pump and flush blood through veins
another day. I fill my lungs, and empty them.
Birds accompany me with whistles and tweets
singing, *Semi-sweet. Semi-sweet.*

Where I Stand

Ah. At long last, the ocean again.
After a parading march of seasons without.
Taurus (earth sign), land lubber, grounded on shore,
looking out at the vast while digging toes in,
I'm fed by the waves' sound, their reach, their power.
The way white clouds hang above,
looking like gulls frozen in flight,
as the gulls themselves soar and swoop.
Rush and recede lulls in an endless loop.
Children play, surfers surf, sun worshipers
lay with faces turned to warmth
like morning glory blossoms in early day.
The fabric of sounds, rhythmic and lush,
forms a background intricate yet whole, coherent,
a foley artist's craftwork, sounds and visuals in concert,
telling a story of this magical, liminal space,
where water meets land and they dance
and dance and dance. Surf and sand laced
and ruffled with seaweed and breezes.
A dynamic of seen and unseen.
Hints of a grand scheme.
Light glints on surfaces in relation, in motion.
Rolling swells, smooth shells, sparkling shore
softening, receiving the imprint where I stand.

Morning Walk

Lacey seaweed, green on the tan shore,
making rows of curves, fringing the water
like a scalloped lampshade's edge.

Sparkling shells, the moon-shimmers,
translucent disks some name "toenails"
sprinkle shore line sand where the tide has pushed them,
mapping out their own glittering galaxy,
later to be criss-crossed by footprints
of beach combers, and gulls.

Where the waves ride the sandbar,
they are line after line of charging white horses,
engaged in battle, kicking dust at their feet.

Shall I join them?

Horseshoe Crab

Old wise one,
keeper of ancient ways.

How did you appear here, on
this peopled shore?

Like a messenger from another planet,
exotic, startling as a moose!

Old wise one,
carrying others on it's back.

A village of shelled creatures,
hangers on, attached, hitchhiking a ride.

Old armored one with
dark shell, spiked tail protruding,

do our hearts run on the same pulse-
beat, hearing the same song?

Where have you been?
Where do you go?

How have you remained so long?
Why do I wish you well?

I bid you safe journey.
Imagine the stories you can tell!

Returning Tide

The tide, coming in, pushes up neat clumps
of seaweed, glistening green, like the "grass"
dumped from an easter basket.

Waves roll in with a gentle power, pushing the
last line of sand-wetting water higher, higher,
up onto the beach.

The sandbar is well covered now. Sandcastles
once dug and packed, returning to original form.
My shadow grows longer and I'm forced to
retreat, and retreat again, giving up ground
to the encroaching waves.

The sound of the surf will be in my sleep tonight.

Pearl Lustered Kiss

Grey, white, baby blue;
sea of teal below.

Surfers, bobbing, wait their turn.
They'll ride a wave's curl to shore.

High above, inside pearl-lustered mist,
a silver-grey glinting dog frolics.

Walking speckled sand, look up
once more to see the show.

A pale cricket travels now,
astride magic carpet-cloud.

This too will morph, I know,
as blowing breezes kiss and flow.

Dusk

So like a blanket gently laid
On evening's shoulders
Cooler air settles in, tucked
Under the chin of twilight

Birds announce it
Peepers chirp their pips
Young children need one last stroll,
Dogs one last sniff

Garden blossoms revert
Curling back into buds
Insects fly on patrol,
Not knowing bats await them

The air is expectant,
Full of ritual
Clearing way for stars
It's a changing of the guards

Hampton Beach with Rob

At the beach, time changes.
It spreads out, and rolls with the waves,
skims across surface of sand and sea.

It tumbles rocks til smooth.
It holds seagulls aloft.
Time at the beach is endless. Eternal.

Walking the shore takes no time at all.
Yet, all time stills.
The rocks, smooth and shiny, are countless.

The surf relentless.
No matter if gentle or rough,
it is forever.

Tail feather clouds above us. A bird dives
into the waves. I will fill my pocket
with silky stones sculpted in returning tides.

Summoning What Is Dear

I like to wear abalone's shell at my ear.
A drop that hangs from silver,
its glimmer holding all
of ocean's wonder;
all of *smell* and *feel* and *hear*.

Above pebbled shores,
gulls float and surf the air,
time-and-swell-softened treasure is found
alongside purple jellyfish splayed
near sandy seaweed strands and gnarls.
Fluted clamshell crescents, crabs,
translucent green sea glass, twist-shaped driftwood.
Flat disc sand dollars, stamped with a star,
secretly carrying tiny white doves.
Speedy sandpipers with spindly legs racing
salty waves' endless charge-and-retreat.

A trick I do carries all this
for me. Summoning what is dear,
I wear a shard of shimmer,
once home to soft-bodied creature,
held close, precious, iridescent,
dangling as a promise,
open as can be.

Each Flower and Its Bee

Aren't we all,
under each layer
of this, and that, searching
for authentic voice?
The un-dictated one. The one
generating organically, from truth.
Our truth. Unique
to us. Born
of our particular
circumstances.
Our road; our path;
our steps; our stumbles.
Recoveries. Discoveries.
Creations. Destructions.
Where and how we blend
with the natural world,
see the stars,
hear the birds,
smell the earth,
value each step
as a resting ground.
Love each flower and its bee
as sweet treasure
that feeds us.

Bedazzled

I step into the arms of the day and
like a casket at a wake,
or a book to its marked page,
this morning's sky opens its lid of grey
just enough to reveal
all the colors layered there.

Slit like a lolling lizard's eye,
parting to see what lies ahead,
gray cloud gaps open, revealing
pearly creams and baby blues lustered inside.

Oh, this peek under the bed; this lift of veil!
Opened sky now blushes,
the way abalone secrets shimmer a shell.
Iridescent nacre speaking its magic,
glimmered pink blessings unfold before my heart.
Day sings its song of fullness, arms open
in a beckoning call to embrace, engage, celebrate, revere.

I am a sponge, saturating in wonder.
Today's lifting lid offers all that is needed.
Soaked in its spell, a cast of bedazzlement,
I carry this forward.
How long will it last?

Twirling

So much fuss about Barbie Doll,
while, off Cape Cod Great White sharks
leap to chomp sea bass from fishing poles.
An aggressive California sea otter
confiscates surfer's boards.
In Russia's war on Ukraine, Transfiguration Cathedral
is tragically transformed, rubbled by raining bombs.
Thieving politicians plot to steal more power,
wielding greed and gluttony, corruption coating them
in souring suits of rot and filth.

Our planet spins on its axis still,
the seasons change as practiced,
but all is cracking up, bulging out, tipping over,
calving off, burning, flooding, wheezing
through thick fog of discord.

Fly away fast little birds, take seeds & nuts
as you can find them.
Swoop swallows, acrobatic in sky's blue,
above the lake where you play.
Flutter leaves, fringing branches
on graceful trees that gird us.
Do your dance. Dance and dance while music is playing.
Let stars come out and shine
with a moon watching, amused, glowing.
Bask in the light of that silver disk,
gaze aloft at this night sky,
wander and dwell in wonder, risking the not-knowing,
twirl under a spell of uncertainty.
Surely, there'll be a path to see, eventually?

In my wildest

poetry dreams, I am invited to join
Matthew Olzmann's writing group.
We form a small circle of locals,
non-competitive, encouraging and enthusiastic,
meeting to share creative work.

In my wildest political dreams, justice is brought
for crimes of corruption and exploitation.
And in my wildest dreams for society,
"we are all in this together" really *means*
there's no great poverty, no grandiose wealth;
we help each other cover the necessities
for survival, and good health.

In my wildest dreams for the planet, Earth survives
our era of mass neglect and ruin. We live in harmony;
thriving ecosystems, with their balanced heat and rain,
sustain us, and Earth loves us again.

In my wildest flower dreams,
I weave through flourishing fields
in waves of echinacea, aster, clover, phlox.
Bees and butterflies dance in the buttercups,
and I am gleeful, grateful, for the perfect blue of forget-me-nots.

Cycle

Everything hinges on the way
aster blossoms pop up purple,
above the dried milkweed in an October field.

A purple to pierce the heart,
or rather, make it jump in its ribbed cage,
lifted to a ribald Morris dance, its pulse

rejoicing at each tint and tinge.
Sumac leaves, flaming red, singe the backdrop sky.
Pointed flags, they warn of deep sleep to come.

Make sure it is sleep, says red, says orange,
and not death. Take care
this raging is a party to wake up from—

bells jing-jangling again, assured we've paid attention
to foundations of renewal—
allowing us survival; to start again, sustained.

Post-It Note

Today as I walked, I wondered—what is that
brilliant version of red I see, dotting the path
in front of me?
Little love notes dropped from high
above, from the Maple tree? Post-it notes
have fluttered down from a leafy canopy.
Reminders to remember. *Attention, attention.*
Little bird chirps come from the purple aster,
crows caw in the pines, a chipmunk pips
from the elm tree trunk. Announcements reverberate.
Remember this is cycle, not time to be afraid.
Is that the message wafted my way
in what seems some sort of pivotal day?
Autumnal Equinox marks tomorrow.
There may be loneliness in our future;
there may be sorrow. What to do besides carry on,
take the walk, hear the birds,
hug the ones we can, remember ones we cannot.
I have seen many winters come by now,
many turns from this to that.
Only way I have learned to weather uncertainty:
find the constant, sink into the core. And love
the beauty. Notice how it is always present,
whether in back, or fore ground.
We carry love that abounds. More vast than our bodies,
small beating muscle of heart in a chest.
This body is a shell afloat in the larger sea,
only a temporary container of me.

What I Ask

Let me meet this day
on its own terms
and let it greet me
on mine.

Together, we will circle each other,
slowly and with tenderness,
with intention and attention.
Gradually, eventually, we'll be in step,

dancing a dance
to the rhythms that surround us,
that hold us to each other,
as we dip and swivel, travel and twirl.

Let me be the pearl, worn shiny
and lustrous with time and grit, inviting
my own unique light to emit
so I might step with confidence and love

and an understanding
of preciousness.
Let me greet this day as it comes,
and let it hold me in caring arms.

About the Author

Marjorie Moorhead writes from a river valley, surrounded by mountains and four season change, at the border of NH/VT. She found a voice in poetry after surviving AIDS in its early years, and becoming a mother. Much of her work addresses survival, environment, relationship, and appreciation of the everyday.

She is author of *Every Small Breeze* (Kelsay Books 2023), the chapbooks *Survival: Trees, Tides, Song* (Finishing Line Press, 2019), *Survival Part 2: Trees, Birds, Ocean, Bees* (Duck Lake Books, 2020), and *In My Locket* (Finishing Line Press 2024). Her poems have appeared in journals including *Amethyst Review, Tiny Seed Literary, Moist Poetry Journal, Bloodroot Literary, Sheila-Na-Gig, Porter House Review, Poeming Pigeon, Verse-Virtual, What Rough Beast, A River Sings, The Poet's Touchstone*, and others. Her poems are included in a large number of anthologies, including those that benefit environmental, women's, Covid first-responder, and refugee aid organizations. She is proud to have a poem included in *The Wonder of Small Things, Poems of Peace & Renewal* (James Crews, ed. 2023). She has had poems nominated for Pushcart Prize, and Best of the Net.

Marjorie's local poetry group is 4th Friday Poets, a small group that has been meeting twice a month for years. In summer of 2019 Marjorie enjoyed a workshop at Fine Arts Work Center, Provincetown MA, during their poetry week, thanks to a tuition scholarship from Indolent Books. She has attended many readings and workshops online with some amazing and inspiring poets, thanks to zoom. Love of family, daily walks in each season, tai chi practice, and poetry community are the things that feed her.

www.ingramcontent.com/pod-product-compliance
Lightning Source LLC
Chambersburg PA
CBHW030911170426
43193CB00009BA/811